KEEPSAKE CRAFTS

CANDLES

KEEPSAKE CRAFTS

CANDLES

PAMELA WESTLAND

SUNSET PUBLISHING CORPORATION
MENLO PARK, CALIFORNIA

A QUARTO BOOK

First Printing June 1995

Copyright © 1995 Quarto Inc.
Published by Sunset Publishing Corporation,
Menlo Park, CA 94025

First edition. All rights reserved, including the
right of reproduction in whole or in part in any
form.

ISBN 0-376-04260-5

Reprinted 1995

Library of Congress Catalog Card Number:
94-068454

For more information on Keepsake Crafts
Candles or any other Sunset Book, call
1-800-634-3095.

This book was designed and produced by
Quarto Inc.
The Old Brewery
6 Blundell Street
London N7 9BH

Editor Joanne Jessop
Managing editor Anna Clarkson
Designers Peter Bridgewater /
Ron Bryant-Funnell
Photographer Nelson Hargreaves
Illustrator Tony Masero
Art director Moira Clinch
Editorial director Sophie Collins

Manufactured in Hong Kong by
Regent Publishing Services Ltd
Printed in China by
Leefung-Asco Printers Ltd

CONTENTS

INTRODUCTION

The gentle, flickering, and friendly glow of candlelight has come to symbolize friendship and festivity. The intimate pool of golden light created as a focal point for a romantic dinner; the cluster of beeswax candles shining more brightly as daylight fades into dusk; the festive flickering of candles at holiday times – some of the most significant and memorable occasions in our lives are enhanced by the presence of candles.

In many parts of the world candles were the main source of artificial light until the comparatively recent advent of gas and electricity. From earliest times, candles and tapers were made by dipping rushes into tallow (an animal fat derived from sheep, pigs and cows), beeswax, or spermaceti (wax obtained from the sperm whale). It was only in the mid-nineteenth century that paraffin wax was first extracted from crude oil. The technique of molding candles, which now enables us to produce so many decorative and representational shapes, had been invented centuries before, in Paris in the fifteenth century.

or rolling a sheet of honeycomb beeswax around a length of wick, the enthusiastic amateur is encouraged to experiment with dyes and scented oils, with paints and applied decorations, and with imaginative displays.

The craft of candlemaking, with its long history and strong traditions, is one that offers creative opportunities to people with varying levels of artistic ability. After first experiencing the almost certain satisfaction of turning a colorless candle out of an improvised or ready-made mold

Successive sections in this book explain the basic materials and techniques you will need, then explore some of the delightful and unusual designs you can create by using rigid and flexible molds of all kinds. These decorations include deep purple candles scented with crushed lavender flowers, mosaic candles created from leftovers of colored wax, fish-shaped candles set in metal molds, and candles molded in bundt pans. Chunks of ice are used to create textured candles with a random series of holes, and cinnamon sticks are embedded in ice-blue candles for the most aromatic offerings ever.

The technique of rolling and molding beeswax, so simple that it is literally child's play, fires the imagination for decorative ways to display the candles. Chubby, textured candles set in dough rings; slender dinner candles contrasted with bright shiny brass holders and glossy evergreens; hive-shaped candle domes embellished with insect shapes; harvest and Thanksgiving arrangements combining seasonal vegetables and honeycomb candles – there are plenty of ideas for decorations the year around.

Decorating candles that you make or buy promises just as much craft satisfaction and at least as many decorative possibilities. You may want to embellish plain candles with studs or shells, buttons or beads, pressed flowers or spices; paint them with heavy texture or elegant shapes; or surround them with garlands of flowers and ribbons. Whatever your preference, you will find that you have more than enough choices.

MATERIALS

You can turn back the clock and produce effective and attractive candles with nothing more specialized than melted wax and a wick. But to increase your satisfaction in the craft, and the range and shape of your designs, you may want to experiment with molds, dyes, and a few other pieces of equipment. Your candle workshop could be an undisturbed corner of the kitchen or a gas burner on the patio. The illustrations show some of the equipment you will find helpful.

WICKS AND WICKING NEEDLES

Unlike the "rush dips" of Roman times, which were made of peeled rushes, present-day wicks are made of braided cotton chemically treated to improve its ability to burn. They are available in a range of thicknesses in round section (most suitable for use in beeswax candles and tall pillar candles) and flat section.

DECORATIONS

Pressed flowers and leaves, flat glass marbles, pearl buttons and beads, gold braid and whole spices – there is no end to the range of decorations you can add to or incorporate in your candle designs.

RIGID MOLDS

Ready-made molds in clear or opaque plastic and in metal come in a wide range of shapes and sizes. Choose from cylindrical or square, pyramid or cone-shaped, hexagonal and spherical molds. They all have a hole for the wick, and a firm base so that they will stand level.

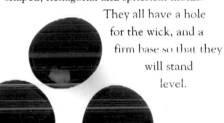

WAXES

Uncolored paraffin wax is sold in various forms: as a large solid block, small cylinders, or easy-to-use flakes. Stearic acid, or stearin, used as a hardener, comes in small cylinders or flakes. Beeswax, an entirely natural product, is sold in block form to make molded candles of all kinds; the blocks are shades of untreated brown or bleached white. Beeswax is also sold in rolled sheets, in natural or dyed colors, to make hand-rolled candles.

CANDLE DYES

Think of a color and you can achieve it with the use of wax-soluble dyes. They are usually sold in the form of disks or "buds," which can be cut or scraped for use with small quantities of melted wax.

FLEXIBLE MOLDS

These are the ones you need for creating candles in a variety of representational shapes; for example, pieces of fruit, Christmas trees, pine cones and nursery-rhyme characters.

MAKING YOUR OWN CANDLES

A basket of fruit-shaped candles as appealing and colorful as any display of oranges and lemons, apples and pears; a school of pearly-white and deep-sea-blue candles set in oyster shells; a cluster of rolled honeycomb beeswax candles with their characteristic waffle-like texture and sweet, subtle aroma – in time you will surely want to make them all. But whichever candles you aspire to make first, you will achieve the best results by following a few simple, basic rules.

THE MATERIALS

At the heart of every candle is a wick, the means by which the liquid wax is carried to the flame. Choose the wick according to the size of candle you intend to make. Braided cotton wicks are sold in sizes described by the diameter of the candles for which they are best suited. For example, a half-inch wick is suitable for use with a candle that is half an inch in diameter.

Flat braided wicks are most commonly used, although round ones, which have a greater density, are recommended for use with beeswax candles and large, thick pillar candles.

Paraffin wax, an odorless wax that is a by-product of the oil refining process, is widely available, and because of its lack of color can be dyed to any required tint or shade, however light or dark. The wax is solid at normal room temperature, and melts between 135°F and 140°F. It is usual to add up to 10 percent stearin, or stearic acid, when using paraffin wax for candlemaking; in some cases the wax is sold already mixed with stearin, which both hardens the wax and slows down the burning rate. The addition of stearin is not recommended, however, when using flexible rubber molds because it tends to rot the surface.

Beeswax, too, both hardens the wax and increases the burning time.

Many church candles are made with a one-in-four proportion of beeswax and paraffin wax. A natural product of the hive, beeswax can be used alone to make long-lasting candles with a sweet scent. It is sold in block form, from which molded candles can be made, and, more commonly, in thinly rolled sheets. Cut to the required length and with a wick inserted, these beeswax sheets can be rolled in minutes to make the traditional highly textured honeycomb candles.

Although you can color wax with any wax-soluble substances such as poster paints and wax crayons, ready-made wax dyes are the easiest to control. They are sold in disk or bud form and are usually used in the proportion of ¼ ounce to 4½ pounds of wax. To use the dye in smaller quantities, or to dilute or intensify the

color, it is best to add it gradually to the melted wax and then allow a little to harden on a cold saucer. Only when it has set will you be able to judge the color of the finished candle.

MAKING MOLDED CANDLES

1 Lightly brush a flexible or rigid mold with clear vegetable oil (do not use extra virgin olive oil, which is cloudy) and blot any excess with some paper towel.

2 Thread the appropriate wick into a wicking needle and thread it through the hole in a rigid mold. Flexible molds do not normally have a prepared hole, so it will be necessary to pierce one.

3 Release the wick from the needle, allowing about an inch extra, and seal around the hole with mold seal or the tacky clay used by florists.

4 Suspend the wick vertically in the mold by tying it to a wick rod, a split cane, or a toothpick. Cut off excess wick and stand or balance the mold in an upright position.

5 Melt the wax in a double boiler or a bowl over a pan of simmering water. Stir in the

stearin, if you are using it, and any wax dye until it is evenly distributed.

6 Pour the melted wax into the mold and allow it to settle. When a well has formed around the wick, carefully top off with more melted wax and allow it to harden overnight.

To release the candle from a rigid mold, invert it and give it a gentle tap. Carefully peel off a flexible mold, starting at the top and easing the mold gently all around the candle.

FRUIT BASKET

Rosy apples and ripe pears, tangy oranges and lemons and luscious-looking bunches of grapes – this cheerful candle collection is made using flexible molds you can buy in craft shops.

Make these fruit-shaped candles in fantasy or realistic colors, and if you wish, use acrylic paints to add characteristic color variations. For instance, a patch of rosy red paint, smudged at the edges, turns a sour-looking apple into one that is far more appealing.

When the wax has hardened and the paint is thoroughly dry, polish the fruit pieces using a soft cloth and a few drops of vegetable oil.

Display these lovely fruit candles in a basket lined with contrasting green leaves in a fruit bowl or on a flat dish, piled high in pyramid fashion. When the lights are low, issue a friendly warning to guests – do not attempt to eat the decorations!

Add refreshingly scented citrus oils to the wax for the orange- and lemon-shaped candles or, if you plan to use them outdoors, add citronella oil to keep the bugs away.

SWEET LAVENDER

These dark lavender-colored candles have the sweetest scents of all —

the fragrance of dried lavender flowers blended with the wax. Light one

to give off a subtle aroma in the living room or a romantic aura in

the bedroom.

To make these scented candles, lightly crush dried lavender flowers with a pestle and mortar, or beat them gently with one end of a rolling pin. Be careful not to crush the lavender flowers to a fine powder. Use a blend of blue and red dyes, or a deep violet dye, to color the wax. First, let a little set on a cold saucer to check that you like the shade. To make the darker block candle shown here, pour the melted wax into the prepared square mold; when it is on the point of setting, sprinkle on the crushed lavender flowers. Use a thin wooden stick or a metal skewer to stir them in and distribute them evenly throughout the wax. For a lighter, less dense effect, whisk the melted colored wax with a whisk or an electric mixer. Pour the frothy wax into the prepared mold and, just before it sets, stir in the lavender flowers.

These dinner candles in various colors from pale lavender blue to deep mulberry are scented with lavender oil. They can be displayed in elegant silver or crystal holders, or for a romantic effect, clustered together and tied with gossamer ribbon.

ICE COOL

These highly textured candles are bubbly on the surface and randomly pitted with holes. They are made by a quick-and-easy, fun technique that is applied physics in its lightest form!

To make these "ice candles," insert a slender candle or a taper into a rigid mold of any size or shape. Thread the exposed end of the candle wick through the hole in the mold (do not seal it with mold seal) and stand the mold in a bowl or dish. Then pack the mold with crushed ice or chunks of solid ice. The more ice you use and the larger the chunks, the larger the holes in the candle will be. Now melt, then pour on some melted wax. As it cools, the wax forms a thin skin around the pieces of ice, which will determine the texture of the candle. And as the ice melts and the water runs out of the hole in the base of the mold, it will leave its mark behind – a random pattern of holes in the finished candle.

Children especially like to experiment with this type of candlemaking. They are fascinated to watch the transformation as melted wax and solid ice are changed into solid wax and liquid water. Where young children are concerned, be sure to supervise when the melted wax is poured.

MOSAIC PATTERNS

Pink and blue, orange and violet, yellow and green – color them as you will. These mosaic

candles are made by a simple technique suitable for use in any rigid mold.

To make mosaic candles, thread the wick in the mold in the usual way and seal the hole. Then pack the mold with random chunks of colored wax, pressing them as close as possible against the sides so that the colors will be seen at their brightest.

For the mosaic effect, you can use chunks of wax in a single color or in a combination of two or more colors. You can even use leftover candle ends in this delightfully thrifty way. (To avoid a criss-cross confusion of wicks as the mosaic candle burns down, pull out and discard short pieces of wick in used candle ends.)

Pour on melted white wax to fill in all the spaces and tap the mold sharply on the working surface to settle the wax. Pour on more wax until the surface is level.

If you are color coordinating candles to match your furnishings or a table theme, remember that the coating of clear wax will dilute the color of the candle chunks inside.

PERFECT CATCH

Make a school of colorful fish-shaped candles to decorate the table for

a poolside party, or create a miniature pond of floating fish candles as

an indoor table centerpiece.

These fish candles can be made in small metal molds, sold in kitchen shops to shape fish mousses or molded gelatin. Or you could shape your own molds using a double thickness of heavy-duty aluminum foil. The candles shown here are about 5 inches long.

To evoke the atmosphere of a brilliant school of tropical fish, make your collection as colorful and exotic as you please. It is a good idea to mold one fish candle each time you are coloring wax for another project.

Brush the molds lightly with vegetable oil for easy release and tip out the shapes when the wax has hardened. Dip a length of wick into melted wax to stiffen it, pierce two holes in each fish shape with a heated metal skewer and insert short pieces of wick into the holes. To add a realistic shimmer to the exotic fish shapes, brush the candle surface all over with a gold metallic acrylic paint.

CANDLE RING

Plain or colored candle wax set in a ring-mold pan has all the makings of

a party centerpiece. You can decorate the outside of the ring with pressed

flowers, leaves, and grasses. For a pretty see-through effect, stand a small

candle in the center.

For a smooth wax surface to decorate with pressed plant materials, choose a ring mold or a bundt pan with plain sides when making a candle ring.

Brush the inside of the mold evenly with vegetable oil and use paper towels to blot off any that has settled in the base. Excess oil discolors and clouds the wax. Pour in melted wax, and when it has settled, pour in more to level the surface.

When the wax has set, release it from the mold. Dip a length of wick into melted wax, pierce four holes around the top of the ring with a hot metal skewer and insert four pieces of wick. Add melted wax to fill in around the wicks.

Create the flower pattern around the ring. Choose your flowers to suit the season or the mood of the occasion.

The white candle ornamental grasses, ring is decorated lady's mantle and with a delicate tiny alyssum tracery of pressed flowers.

Feathery love-in-a-mist and bright blue Iberian crane's-bill flowers were pressed into decorative service around this ice-blue candle ring.

Experiment with several variations: use even-sized flower heads to compose a geometric or an abstract pattern; arrange flowers and slender leaves into a bouquet; or position flower stems to simulate the way they grow. Use melted-candle glue to stick the materials in place. Do not add too much dye to the wax. The deeper the color, the less translucent the candle.

21

Whether your molds are family heirlooms or come with your favorite supermarket mousse, you can have fun with them and a few acrylic paints, transforming homemade candles into works of art.

Some shapes look good with a build-up of several layers of paint, giving the candle a solid, architectural appearance. Others look best with a very light coat of paint applied with an almost dry brush. And some shapes take equally well to either treatment.

The stone-like candle on the right was painted with a blend of black and white acrylic paints, mixed to a deep shade of gray. When the paint was thoroughly dry the arches, recesses and geometric patterns on the top were highlighted with gold metallic paint in the same medium.

By contrast, the pretty candle on the left was lightly brushed with gold acrylic paint to give it an ethereal, translucent look.

A small mold with a bunch of grapes at the top was used to turn out an expensive-looking candle that would flatter individual place-settings.

The molded candle was first brushed with green acrylic paint and then given a sheer coating of gold metallic paint for a translucent effect.

KITCHEN ARTISTRY

These candles were all shaped in pottery molds from the

kitchen shelves. The final results show what an

impression you can make with just a

brushful of acrylic paint!

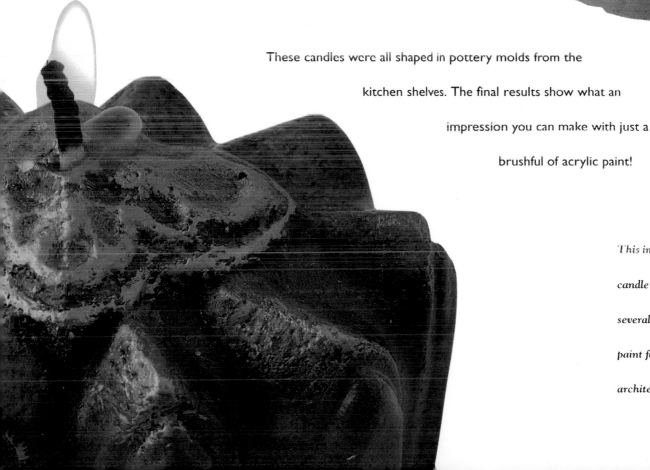

This impressive

candle was given

several layers of

paint for a solid

architectural look.

FALL LEAVES

The fallen leaves of early autumn gathered from the forests and the herb garden can all be arranged to embellish plain candles that you buy or make yourself. It is a delightful way to add a seasonal note to your table decorations.

Gather a selection of shapely and colorful leaves and press them between sheets of paper toweling under heavy pressure. Once they are dry, you will have a wealth of decorative materials to enhance plain candles of all shapes and sizes – thick pillar candles, slender dinner candles, or short, squat candles.

Sort through your pressed leaves and grade them according to size. Arrange a selection of leaves around the candle and adjust them into a pleasing pattern. For example, you might like to position a cluster of golden maple leaves to look as if they are floating down from the tree, or position purple-tinted chervil leaves so that each one is seen in stark silhouette.

Once you have arranged the leaves, run a thin line of melted clear glue around the edges and along the stems, and press them in place. Hold a piece of paper over the leaves to help press down the edges without damaging them.

With the light of
the candle behind
them, the leaves are
seen in all their
intricate detail.

NICE & SPICY

These pale blue candles have more than just a hint of spice — they

have sticks and sticks of it, in the form of cinnamon sticks

beneath the surface of the wax.

This is a technique you can use with any straight-sided rigid mold; a cylindrical or square, rectangular, or even conical mold will do. Depending on the size of the mold, use whole cinnamon sticks, in their tightly furled rolls, or split them vertically with a very sharp knife and use slivers and shavings. You will need to slit them and shape the slivers when using conical or pyramid-shaped molds, which are narrow at the top.

Cut the cinnamon sticks or slivers to the full depth of the mold. Melt the wax and, if you wish, add a little dye to make it just off-white. But remember, too much dye will take away the natural translucent quality of the wax and hide the cinnamon sticks from view.

Lightly oil the mold, pour in a little melted wax and tip the mold so that the wax covers one side with a thin, even film. Position the cinnamon sticks as quickly as possible by pushing them into the soft wax.

Pour in a little more wax to cover another section of the mold, press more cinnamon into place and continue all around the mold.

Thread a length of wick through the hole in the mold, seal it with mold seal and pour in melted wax to fill the cavity.

When you turn out the spiced candles, be prepared for them to have a somewhat rugged appearance — it is all part of their charm! Cinnamon sticks, among the most aromatic of whole spices, contribute a heady fragrance to molded candles.

To make an egg-shaped candle with the wax fully exposed, break away a small part of an eggshell at the flat end. Tip out the egg and wash and drain the shell. Let it dry in a warm place.

Brush the inside of the eggshell with vegetable oil (this makes it easier to peel away the shell later) and thread a darning needle with a piece of thin wick. Gently pierce a hole in the shell at the pointed end and thread the wick through it. Seal the hole at the pointed end with mold seal, secure the wick and stand the shell in an eggcup. Carefully pour in wax to fill the shell and allow it to set.

When the wax is hard, gently crack the eggshell and peel it away. Polish the egg-shaped candle with a few drops of vegetable oil on a soft cloth.

SHELLING OUT

Eggshells are so ideal as candle molds that they might have been designed for just this purpose.

Use egg-shaped candles in one of two ways: crack away the shells to expose the wax shapes; or

leave the shells on as the most natural containers of all.

Colorful egg candles make a perfect table centerpiece for Sunday brunch.

SIMPLE ROLL UPS

Roll beeswax sheets, natural or dyed, into long and short, thick and thin cylinders to create a forest of sweet, honey-smelling candles. Display them all in one color or in a bright medley of mixed hues.

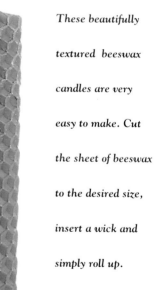

These beautifully textured beeswax candles are very easy to make. Cut the sheet of beeswax to the desired size, insert a wick and simply roll up.

When your display is made up of candles in all shapes and sizes, and particularly if they are multicolored as well, it is a good idea to make them with one common factor to give them unity.

Cut the beeswax sheets into rectangles so that all the candles have straight tops or into shapes with one sloping side so that all the candles have graduated tops. To do this, place the wick along the longer edge and roll toward the shorter edge. Display the candles in clusters on a wooden board laced with ivy trails or in a shallow basket lined with evergreens.

Most craft shops sell sheets of beeswax in its natural color and in red and green. Other more subtle shades may be more difficult to find but are worth seeking out.

Bundles of beeswax candles tied with string, raffia, or cord make a decorative feature in the Shaker tradition.

STRAIGHT FROM THE HIVE

Shape warm beeswax in your hands as if it were clay, or melt it and pour it into flexible molds. Either way, it can fire your imagination and help you come up with a honey of an idea for candles with flair.

If you or the children have mastered the art of clay modeling then you have the skill you need at your fingertips to shape and model beeswax.

You may be able to buy beeswax from a local beekeeper. Or you can save ends of old beeswax candles, unroll them to remove the wicks and melt them in a double boiler or in a bowl placed over a pan of just simmering water.

When the wax has cooled, but is still pliable, shape it into hives, domes,

trees, animal figures, or whatever you wish. Push a fine skewer into the wax while it is still soft and insert a length of wick that has been dipped in melted wax. Hive shapes can be made from a flexible mold or else modeled by hand. First mold the dome shape of a bee hive, then model pli-able wax into a long thin roll. Coil this around the dome, pressing it gently onto the surface, and make textural markings with a knife. Shape the bees with your fingers and press them onto the hive.

Molds in the characteristic beeswax shape – the flat hexagon – can be bought in some health food stores or made from a double thickness of heavy-duty aluminum foil. Press a corn cob onto the soft wax to give it the identifiable pattern, then make a bee for the top. The ones shown here, highlighted with gold acrylic paint, are reminiscent of the "golden bee" pendant found at ancient Malia, in Crete.

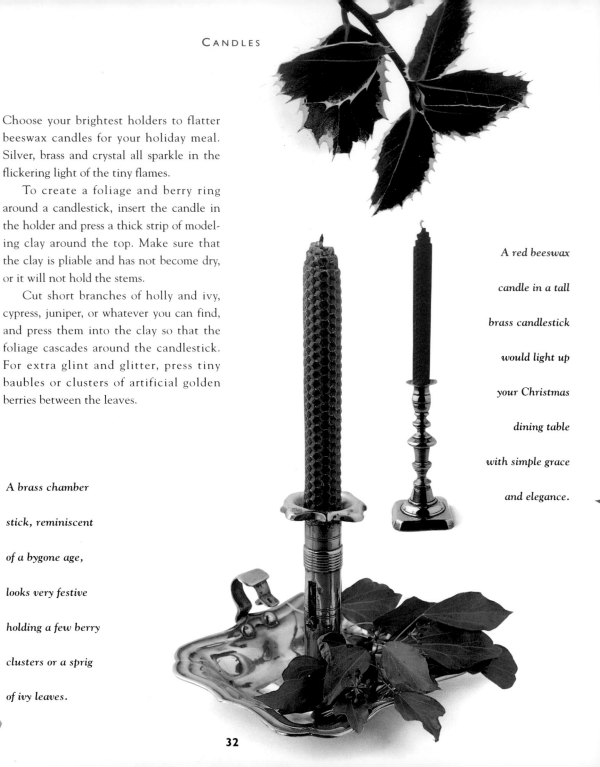

Choose your brightest holders to flatter beeswax candles for your holiday meal. Silver, brass and crystal all sparkle in the flickering light of the tiny flames.

To create a foliage and berry ring around a candlestick, insert the candle in the holder and press a thick strip of modeling clay around the top. Make sure that the clay is pliable and has not become dry, or it will not hold the stems.

Cut short branches of holly and ivy, cypress, juniper, or whatever you can find, and press them into the clay so that the foliage cascades around the candlestick. For extra glint and glitter, press tiny baubles or clusters of artificial golden berries between the leaves.

A brass chamber

stick, reminiscent

of a bygone age,

looks very festive

holding a few berry

clusters or a sprig

of ivy leaves.

A red beeswax

candle in a tall

brass candlestick

would light up

your Christmas

dining table

with simple grace

and elegance.

32

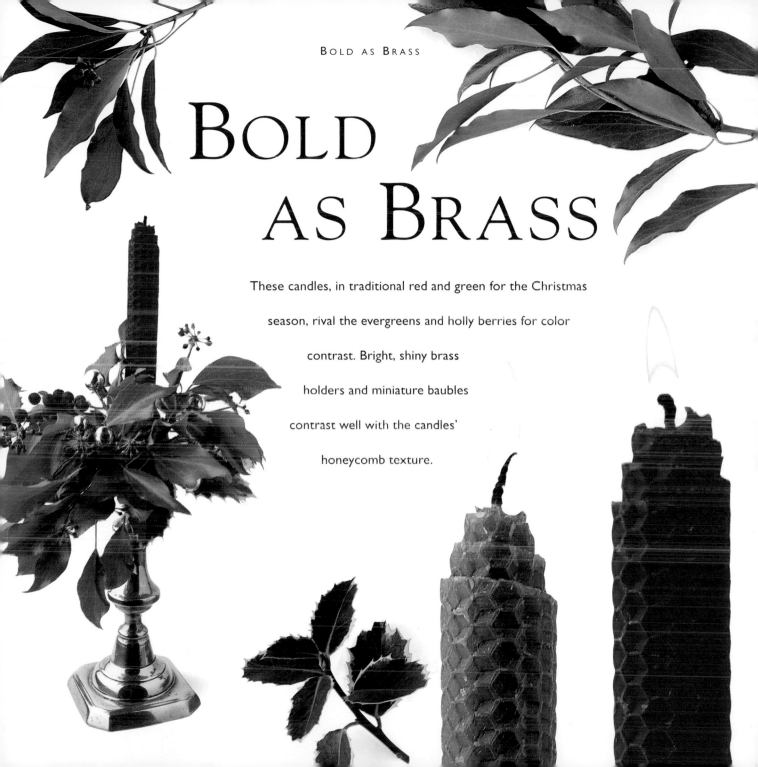

BOLD
AS BRASS

These candles, in traditional red and green for the Christmas

season, rival the evergreens and holly berries for color

contrast. Bright, shiny brass

holders and miniature baubles

contrast well with the candles'

honeycomb texture.

The large dough rings are made from a regular bread dough, glazed with beaten egg and milk and sprinkled with poppy seeds. After normal baking, the rings are left in the oven to continue cooking at a very low temperature until they feel light and sound hollow when tapped.

The smaller dough rings and the star-shaped candleholders are made from salt dough. Acrylic paints were used to color the salt-dough fruits and leaves that decorate the candleholders.

Melted beeswax set in slender cylindrical molds creates beeswax candles with a difference.

DOUGH RINGS

Natural honeycomb candles and toasty-brown dough rings make perfect partners for a homey table setting. Make the rings from your favorite bread dough or from a decorative salt-dough mixture; then, if you like, paint or glaze them.

THANKSGIVING TIME

Honeycomb beeswax in its natural color is perhaps the best choice for a country-style group. Make or buy the candles in a range of heights to add visual interest to an arrangement, and gather together a collection of highly textured or deeply colored vegetables.

Choose squashes of all shapes and sizes – golden nugget squash, acorn squash, custard squash and butternut squash; a cluster of knobby gourds, dried and brushed with a high-gloss varnish; or a softer vegetable option including large tomatoes, eggplants, and red, yellow, and green peppers.

Gather some fallen leaves – maple, chestnut, sycamore, beech – and spray or brush them with a spattering of gold craft paint. They will give the decoration just the extra sparkle a party table deserves.

When the mood is informal, set the party table with sturdy beeswax candles, a cluster of seasonal vegetables, and a scattering of fallen leaves. Your decoration will strike the right note from harvest until Thanksgiving.

UNDERSEA EXPLORATION

For an exciting design concept, explore the possibility of setting plain and

colored candle wax in shells of all kinds. The texture contrasts are terrific.

Sort through any shells you have, select those with the deepest cavities and fill them with candlewax. This is a practical and decorative form of recycling.

Fish restaurateurs often give you their empty oyster shells, just for the asking. Wash, scrub and thoroughly dry them, then pick out those that are most suitable to hold a candle. Some halves may be almost flat and would hold very little wax; other shells may have deep hollows that would accommodate a long-burning candle.

The pale pearly colors of shells perfectly complement the soft glow of the candle. You might prefer to color the wax a deep sea blue to add a marine look to your table setting, or perhaps leave the wax uncolored and virtually indistinguishable from the interior of the shell.

To make shell candles, cut short pieces of wick, stick each one to the inside of a shell with a dab of tacky modeling clay and secure the wick vertically. A wooden toothpick is ideal for this. Stand the shells in a dish of sand or rice to keep them level, then pour in the melted wax and allow it to set.

Deep, dark blue wax inspires an undersea theme that is enlarged by adding seaweed, driftwood, and a variety of shells.

JEWEL COLORS

Baking pans in daisy and star shapes turn out some of the prettiest candles.

Color the wax ruby red, sapphire blue, amethyst, or emerald for a jewel-bright

candle cluster that is perfect for a summer party.

Trying to find some great shapes for your candles? Why not turn to your kitchen cupboards for inspiration. Try baking pans and dessert molds to set candles in the shape of daisies, stars, crescents, hearts and a host of other patterns.

You could also use cookie cutters to add interest and variety to your table decorations. Seasonal cutters of snowmen and Santa Claus and other children's favorites, such as gingerbread men and teddy bears, can be used in a similar way. Place each cutter on a double thickness of heavy-duty aluminum baking foil and carefully fold up the edges of the foil around the cutter shape. Press the foil close against the cutter to avoid leakage.

Whatever mold you use, brush it lightly with vegetable oil and pour in the colored wax. Turn out the shape when the wax has hardened and bore a hole in the center with a fine metal skewer heated over a candle flame. Insert a short piece of wick that has been dipped in melted wax.

There is beauty in numbers in these bright daisy- and star-shaped candles. Display them in a cluster for the most eye-catching effect.

Let your imagination run wild, making these tin can holders as opulent as you dare. First remove the labels and wash and thoroughly dry the cans. Stand them on old newspapers and lightly spray them all around with gold metallic paint. Allow them to dry and, if necessary, spray again. When the paint is thoroughly dry, secure a piece of wick to the base of each can with a small dab of modeling clay. Secure the wick vertically onto a wick rod and pour in melted

Turn used food cans

to glowing account

by painting them

gold, decorating

with odds and ends

of braid and

beads and

filling them

with melted

beeswax.

A perfect match – a gold-painted candle is decorated with gold-thread braid and glittering beads.

beeswax almost to the top of the can. Melt more beeswax and top off the cans when the levels sink.

Decorate the cans with odds and ends of gold braid, shiny beads and sequin trim (the sheet left over when sequins have been pressed out).

Stand metal holders on a heat-proof surface to avoid damage as the candles burn low. Pour out the wax at frequent intervals to avoid spluttering.

PUTTING ON THE STYLE

Stylish enough for any occasion, these holders just love a party!

You do not need serious money to go for gold, glitter, and glitz. These candleholders have come a long way up in the world since their humble origins as pet food cans.

CHRISTMAS-TREE COPSE

Arrange a forest of Christmas-tree candles with all the beauty and mystery of the woods in winter.

There is nothing new about Christmas trees and flickering candles; or is there? These tree-shaped candles in glittering green and gold have added candle-power provided by the slender tapers.

You can buy these shiny bright tree-shaped candles or make them yourself using cookie cutters (see pages 38–39). Use a hand drill with a small gauge drill bit to bore vertical holes in each layer of branches, or

pierce the holes with several applications of a fine metal skewer heated over a candle flame. Cut short pieces of narrow tapers about 5 inches long and insert them into the holes. Because the tapers have a short burning time, reserve them for the highlight of a special occasion. Use them when bringing the Christmas pudding, wreathed in flaming brandy, to the dining table or to draw attention to one of your most spectacular desserts.

You can buy flexible tree-shaped molds to make candles of a completely different character. The frosty green tree shown here was made by mixing together green and pearly white candle dyes and adding to the melted wax.

Golden candles shaped like pine cones have just the right amount of glamour for a winter party. You can buy candles like these in department stores and specialty shops, or you can make them yourself in flexible molds and color them with metallic gold acrylic paint. Arrange natural pine branches along the table with the candles nestling among them for a fantasy setting, or place each pine cone candle on a dish and surround it with spiky twigs of pine needles. Staying with a similar theme, make rings of natural pine cones to use as stands for pine green pillar candles. Select cones of a similar size, measure the diameter of the candle and use a hot glue gun to form one or two rows of cones into a circle large enough to hold the candle.

If you choose to make the pillar candles, try adding a few drops of pine oil to the melted wax.

PINE FOREST

Adopt the scent and shimmer of the pine forest as a theme for your table decorations and you will have a collection of ideas to mix and match throughout the winter season.

Plain or speckled, pine green pillar candles are enhanced by a ring of pine cones around the base.

Golden pine cone candles are perfect decorations for the Christmas table.

THE GALAXY

Reach for the stars with your decoration and display of candles. Buy star-shaped candles and holders and a galaxy of bright sun, moon, and star ornaments, and your table will be a glittering success.

For a heavenly effect, choose candles

in purple and violet, mulberry and

cranberry colors to contrast with bright

golden star holders

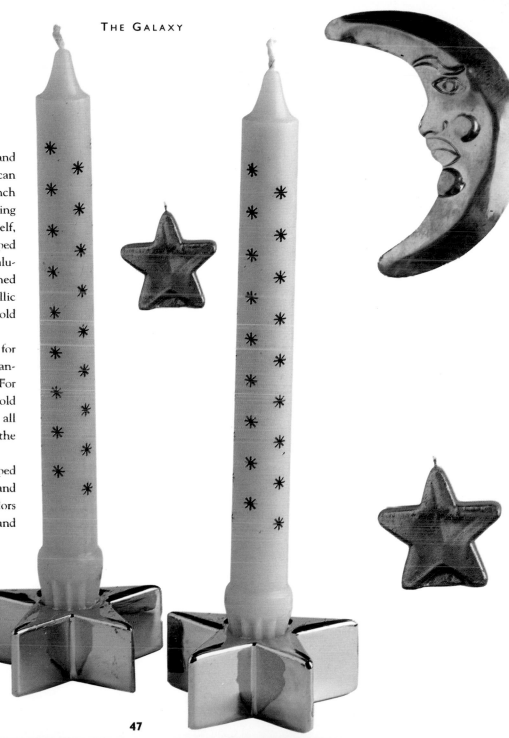

Take the galaxy as your guiding light and give your imagination free rein. You can buy star-shaped candles, about an inch thick, that have been dipped in sparkling gold paint. Or make some for yourself, using star-shaped cookie cutters wrapped in a double thickness of heavy-duty aluminum baking foil. Paint the finished candles with several coats of gold metallic acrylic paint or brush them with gold powder.

Buy plated brass star-shaped holders for a cluster of dinner candles. The cream candles shown here are printed with stars. For a do-it-yourself alternative, stick tiny gold confetti stars (from stationery stores) all over plain candles, or paint or stencil the candles with star shapes.

Look for some sun- and moon-shaped napkin rings and other inexpensive and cheerful ornaments in shiny-bright colors to hang around the "waists" of fat and stubby pillar candles.

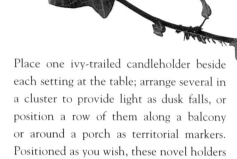

IVY TRAILS

Transform a trio of chunky tumblers into

candle holders for a patio party. All it

takes is a handful of ivy leaves and a

few twists of raffia.

Place one ivy-trailed candleholder beside each setting at the table; arrange several in a cluster to provide light as dusk falls, or position a row of them along a balcony or around a porch as territorial markers. Positioned as you wish, these novel holders will be the shining light at any party.

To make the ivy-leaf holders, select leaves that are of similar size and shape. Position them around the tumblers to check that they fit, then stick them in place with clear quick-setting glue. Braid or twist together several strands of raffia and tie them around the tumbler.

As an alternative, but with a similar theme, twist long strands of small-leaved ivy around the tumblers and secure them discreetly with short pieces of very fine silver wire.

Place a small candle in each holder. You could add a little glamor by using a golden ball-shaped candle.

DECORATIVE STUDWORK

A simple red candle can be smartly dressed up with rows of brass studs.

Bronze and brass studs add texture, style, and interest to plain pillar candles, and lift white household candles into the luxury class.

You may be able to buy studs in specialty shops, where they are sold for leatherwork, or retrieve some from a worn belt. For a look of military precision, measure around the candle and calculate for the same distance between each stud. You may decide to position them about three quarters of an inch or an inch apart. Measure down from the top of the candle and mark pinpoints where the studs are to be, then use a fine skewer to pierce the holes. Press in the studs; be careful to push them in at right angles, otherwise the wax might flake.

Try alternating rows of brass and bronze studs or round-headed studs on solid-colored candles. Tiny brass stud boxes filled with wax make perfect accessories.

50

BAROQUE STYLE

You may choose to arrange the "jewels" at random or place them in neat, measured rows, following the example of the studded candle on the facing page. Make pinpricks to mark the position of the ornaments and stick them on with melted candle glue. It may be necessary to position the jewels one vertical row at a time so that the candle can be placed with that side uppermost until the jewels are secure.

Golden ball-shaped candles look especially rich in shiny "jewelry." Work on small areas at a time and hold the ornaments briefly in place until the glue is firm.

Take a plain gold candle and a handful of flat glass cabochons, shiny glass beads, or cabochon-cut costume jewels. Put the two together and take all the credit for a decoration with the flair and style of centuries past.

51

Whether you dream of the glory of days gone by or simply want to create an effect for a special occasion, these candles have an intriguing aura of history.

ANCIENT LIGHTS

It is easy to imagine candles like these – painted in deep, rich tones and tinged with just a hint of gold – casting their flickering shadows onto old stone walls and medieval manuscripts. The effect is reassuringly easy to achieve.

The antique-looking candles are molded in clear wax and painted with watercolor paints mixed with an added ingredient – green dishwashing liquid – to give the surface of the candles a raised and textured finish.

To achieve this effect, mix the watercolor on a palette or a small dish until it is the color you want. Dilute the paint with a couple of drops of liquid detergent and dab it onto the surface of the candle. A small, flat-ended stippling brush is most suitable for this technique.

Let the paint dry, then spray the surface of the candle evenly with artist's fixative. When this sealant has dried, use a fine-tipped camel-hair brush or any similar type of brush to drizzle on thin wavy lines of gold metallic acrylic paint. Let the paint dry thoroughly before picking up the candle.

Deep, dark colors such as burgundy, midnight blue, and forest green are most effective for these candles, which imitate the deep rich tones and glittering threads of medieval tapestries and silks.

FLORAL GARLANDS

Tall slender altar candles ringed with nosegays of spring and summer flowers and tied with trailing ribbons are delightfully evocative of spring festivals and maypole dances.

Choose some of the prettiest, daintiest flowers you can find – primroses, violets, sweet peas, pinks – and gather them into tiny bouquets. One at a time, hold each bouquet against the surface of a tall plain candle and bind candle and stems together with fine silver wire. Continue around the candle until it is garlanded with flowers; then secure and fasten the wire.

Conceal the wire with a few twists of narrow satin or gossamer ribbon, the prettier the better. Tie the ribbon into a bow with long trailing ends and cut the ends slantwise.

For a bolder approach, and for a wintry look, combine stems of pyracanthus or holly berries with cool-weather annuals; tie them with bows and trailing ribbons in seasonal colors.

CANDLE CLOCK

Be like King Alfred and observe the passing of the hours on a long white candle marked with rings and Roman numerals.

Candles burn at varying rates according to their volume and consistency. Increasing the proportion of beeswax or stearin to melted paraffin wax slows down the burning rate. Some candle manufacturers, especially those who make altar candles for ecclesiastical use, produce a table of the estimated burning times, although these can never be entirely accurate. A candle standing in a draft, for example, will burn down more quickly.

Without accurate information of this kind, you may need to measure the burning rate of a candle similar to the one you propose to decorate as a burning clock. Once you have established the burning rate, mark the candle with black and gold rings of acrylic paint for each hour, then paint on the Roman numerals.

PEARLS OF WISDOM

It is a wise idea to bargain hunt for mother-of-pearl shirt

buttons, strings of pearl beads, and minute seed-pearl

beads. They can all bring a romantic glow to pillar candles

in pretty pastel colors.

Sort through your collection of buttons and beads and grade them according to size. Tiny seed-pearl beads can be used to cover the holes in mother-of-pearl shirt buttons. This is a dainty refinement that will add depth and shape to the applied candle decorations.

Decide on the pattern you want to create around a candle: it may be vertical rows of beads in a staggered pattern, or gentle curves emulating a garland or swag. Lightly mark the proposed pattern on the surface of the candle and stick on the buttons with clear quick-setting glue.

Strings of pearl beads that may have become detached from their clasps can be used to spiral around plain pillar candles or dinner candles with a delightful effect.

To be sure that the spiral is even and regular, pin a piece of thin string to the top of the candle, wind it around and adjust it until the spaces are even. Glue the top of the string of beads close to the string and use it as a guide. Glue the other end of the beads in place and carefully release the string.

Multiple strings of

pearl beads increase

the decorative effect

of the design. Use

pins instead of glue

to fasten heavier

strings of beads to

candles.

Mother-of-pearl

shirt buttons can be

put to good use as

candle decorations.

FRAGRANT STARS

Star anise pods, among the most decorative of seed carriers, have a heady fragrance that is intensified by the gentle heat of the candle flames.

When you buy star anise pods in packages, you will have to pick out all the whole ones and those with stems. Reserve the broken pods for cooking.

Choose pillar candles in suitably "spicy" colors such as paprika, mustard, or cinnamon. Decide on the pattern you wish to create; the pods will vary in size and thickness and do not encourage a precise arrangement. Stick on the pods with melted candle glue or clear quick-setting glue. Try adding a few loose stems for a more rustic effect.

Set light-colored

candle wax in scal-

lop shells;

brush the

candles with

gold powder for

added shimmer.

SHELL CLUSTERS

A ring of contrasting beach-collected shells gives a plain pillar candle some summertime style. A

saucer or platter to match makes an extravagant finishing touch.

The effect of the decoration is almost entirely dependent on your choice of shells. Make your selection as varied as possible in terms of color and texture. Choose some tiny clam shells that are ridged and rugged, and others that are smooth and glossy; some in vibrant seabed colors like coral and oyster pink, and others in muted and

neutral tones of gray and sand. Use clear quick-setting glue to stick a base layer of shells around the candle. Save the showiest ones for the next and more visible layer

Transform an old saucer or platter by sticking on an outer rim of matching shells to complete a seashore duo.

BLACK & GOLD

Black and gold candles, black tableware inlaid with mother-of-pearl, and golden accessories bring glamor to the table.

A tracery of golden ivy leaves painted around slender black dinner candles creates an elegant look that is surprisingly easy to achieve.

You may decide to buy gold-painted candles as the focal point of your table setting. Or, at a fraction of the cost, you may prefer to decorate plain candles as described here.

Gold metallic acrylic paint is the most tenacious medium to use on the hard shiny surface of candlewax. It is possible to apply the paint through a stencil, dabbing it on with a small stippling brush, but it is not easy to lift off the stencil without causing the edges to smear.

With very little practice, even the least accomplished artist is likely to achieve a neater finish by painting on the leaves – a reassuringly simple, near-triangular shape – with a fine-tipped camel-hair or similar paint brush. Practice painting the leaf shapes on a piece of paper, then paint them at random, to wind around the candles. When the paint is dry, add a second coat if necessary.

AN INTERESTING TWIST

Layer upon layer of colored wax is revealed in these sculptured candles as they are carved into twists and folds, bows and spirals.

The craft of hand carving these lovely candles, a tradition in parts of the United States and Northern Europe, is presently enjoying a popular revival on both sides of the Atlantic.

Each candle is built up around a star-shaped core of uncolored wax and stearin set in a ready-made metal mold. The core candle is then dipped into a series of dye vats, each one containing melted wax of a different color. It is the skill of blending the various colors, at least as much as the skill of carving the candle, that creates these traditional works of art.

After the final color-dipping – there may be as many as thirty applications – suspend the candle on a rod while you carve the warm and pliable outer wax into thin slivers. This is not a craft for tentative people because, depending on the humidity and temperature of the room, there may be only five minutes in which to shape the wax.

Trim the wick before lighting it, tip away any melted wax that forms in the well of the candle and limit each burning

session to about one-and-a-half hours for small candles and about three hours for large ones.

After many hours of burning, when you are left with just a decorative and hollow candle shell, insert a smaller, scented household or votive candle into the shell, and

enjoy the intricacy of the carved candle all over again.

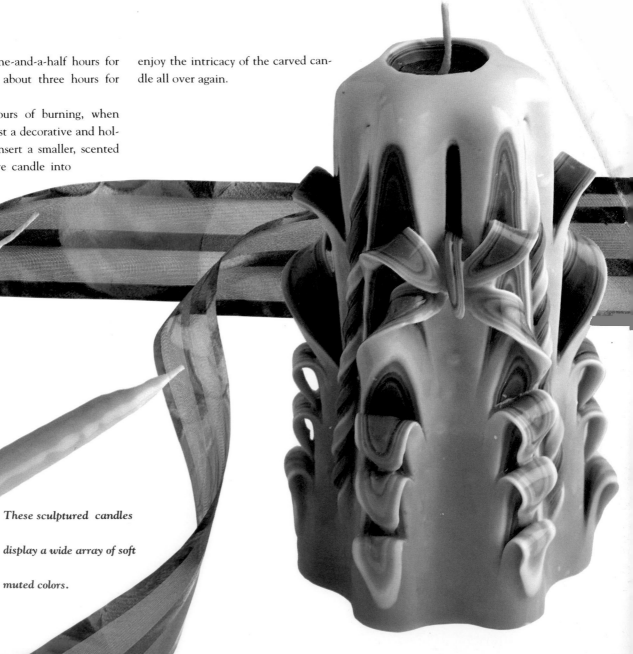

These sculptured candles

display a wide array of soft

muted colors.

ACKNOWLEDGMENTS

We are grateful to the following for supplying so many of the candles shown throughout the book:

Price's Patent Candle Co. Ltd., London, England
Votive candles, pillar candles, dinner candles and novelty candles including stars, Christmas trees and pine cones.

Easy Bee Candles, Gloucestershire, England
Rolled beeswax candle kits, complete with full instructions and template.

The Hand-Crafted Candle Company, Suffolk, England
Hand-crafted dinner candles and pillar candles.